Overcoming:
Faith Food Snack Pack

Faith Lifters that Bless and Build Believers

by
Nick Watson

Nick Watson Prophetic Power Ministries

youcanprophesy@gmail.com

www.youcanprophesy.com

Overcoming:
Faith Food Snack Pack

ISBN 978-0-9943012-1-5

Copyright © by Nick Watson.

All rights reserved. No part of this book may be reproduced or transmitted in any form or by any means, electronic or mechanical, including photocopying and recording or by any information storage and retrieval system, without permission from the author.

Published by Nick Watson Prophetic Power Ministries.

Brisbane. Australia. 4178.

ENDORSEMENTS

Pastor Nick Watson broke new ground with his recent book, "You Can Prophesy - Supernatural. Simple. Safe." The book was straight forward, practical and releasing. His latest book is just as impacting and provides insight and wisdom which if applied will bring release to every person who reads it. As I read the book I was encouraged, inspired and motivated to apply the principles it espouses. I highly recommend you read the book and learn from Pastor Nick's personal understanding of profound scriptural principles.

Wayne Swift

National Leader, Apostolic Church Australia;
Senior Pastor, Church 1330. Scoresby. Victoria. Australia.

Firstly I loved it! – great revelation and content with strong Scriptural foundation and support evidenced right throughout the text. The chapters cover a good diversity of subjects with good use of simple illustrations. I like the application questions and Faith Declarations at the end of each chapter. For me as a preacher, it is certainly a great resource for messages, or preaching thoughts.

Gary Swenson

State Ministries Director,
Australian Christian Churches (previously Assemblies of God)
Queensland and Northern Territory

Nick's book is full of great material and reads well. I'd describe it as a wonderful discipleship tool. I enjoy working through this sort of material with my staff team – it grows big people. Well done!!

Sheridyn Rogers

Senior Pastor, Network Leader, Activate churches, NZ

Nick Watson's new book lives up to its name! I found it very inspiring. You will find your faith lifted as you read each chapter. It is clear that he is not simply an author, but he has been a faithful pastor for decades. That pastoral grace comes through as Nick shepherds you into a stronger, more vibrant faith that works in every-day life. Enjoy reading Overcoming Faith Food Snack Pack as a solidly biblical and practical encouragement to strengthen your faith in Christ!

R. Sonny Misar

Author, "Journey to Authenticity". Senior Pastor, Living Light Church. Winona. Minnesota. USA

Nick's book is not only easy to read but one which is practical, has depth and encourages genuine discipleship. This book contains a good mix of Holy Ghost revelation, biblical fact and principles. This book poses simple yet effective principles of discipleship that will open our lives to God's favour and His anointing.

Chris Wickland

Senior Pastor, Living Word Church. Fareham. England.

As a minister of the Gospel for over 35 years I have learned to value good, sound teaching. So it is with pleasure that I recommend Nick Watson's new book. Nick is a seasoned prophet and pastor that understands the battles and trials we face daily and I believe his book will prove a blessing in practical teaching on overcoming these adversities of life.

Dr. Col Stringer

Author of 20 Christian books, President International Convention of Faith Ministers, Australia.

This book is a Biblical gold mine; written to inform truthfully and experientially its readers with life-changing Biblical principles for an exciting, fruitful, loving obedient, Christ-filled "Life!" Throughout the reading of this easy, comfortable, yet exciting writing style of Nick's, he keeps me turning the pages until I become time and again overcome by the wealth of confirmation and witness in my spirit of the treasure truths that are so beneficially needed in our lives at all times.

Rosemary Renninson

International Devotional Writer/Speaker. Moe. Vic. Australia

This is a book I enjoyed and will refer to again and again. For many years I have studied and taught pastoral ministry and done my best to be a good practitioner. This book would have been so helpful! Nick get this published and I will do my best to get it into as many hands I can.

Philip Underwood

Previously National Leader, Apostolic Churches, New Zealand; Senior Pastor (ret.) Cornerstone Church, Philadelphia. PA. USA

FOREWORD

Reading through this book, my heart rejoiced in the wisdom that came through the pages. This is a book of wisdom - and a gift to all believers, but particularly for those called to ministry. And I believe the Holy Spirit has inspired Nick to write this as an inheritance for the next generation of believers.

With many wonderful quotes and anecdotes, Nick imparts to us the blessing of many lessons learned through his years of ministry experience. There are many keys to be discovered by the reader about how to walk in wisdom. Prompting us with revelations and thought provoking stories, Nick has given us a gift that releases hope and help that, if applied, will cause you to walk in greater wisdom and favour.

One chapter had me "Amen-ing" aloud. Take time to absorb and apply the wonderful truths Nick has to share and you will be better for it!

Katherine Ruonala

Author of "Living in the Miraculous: How God's Love is Expressed Through the Supernatural"
Senior Leader of Glory City Church Brisbane and Apostolic oversight of the the International Glory City Church Network. Founder and Faciliator of the Australian Prophetic Council.
www.katherineruonala.com

DEDICATION

My three dedications of this book are:

- To the Lord Who has partnered with me in many ways to write it.

- To my wife Lynne and our family of four generations.

- To the people who have encouraged me in ministry, so that I can pay-it-forward.

ACKNOWLEDGEMENTS

I thank my amazing wife and the love of my life, Lynne, for being my indispensable partner in life and in ministry.

My thanks also go to all those who have helped me put this book together. Firstly, my chief editor John MacFarlane without whose skills and efforts this book would not have come into reality. Secondly, my proof-reading family and friends Pastor Robert Couper, Elizabeth Scrimshaw, Barbara Hodgman, Lynne Watson and Bronwyn Cunningham.

Special mention and gratitude goes to Lisa Watson of the Printing Well, Wynnum for her sensational design of my book covers and other printing help she donated towards this project. *www.theprintingwell.com.au/*

AUTHOR'S CHOICE

I have made two non-traditional choices in this book. Firstly, I have deleted the definite article "the" from the Name of Holy Spirit, because I want Him to become more personal to my readers. Secondly, I have capitalised a lot of pronouns (such as "Him"), in order to give the Lord the honour He is due and to make clear Who the pronoun represents.

BIBLE QUOTATIONS

Unless stated otherwise, all Bible quotations in this book are taken from:

The Holy Bible, New International Version®, NIV® Copyright © 1973, 1978, 1984, 2011 by Biblica, Inc.® Used by permission. All rights reserved worldwide.

Other versions quoted:

King James Version. Public Domain.

The Amplified Bible. Zondervan Bible Publishers. © 1965. 24th reprinting – April, 1982

Scripture quotations marked ESV are from *The Holy Bible, English Standard Version*® (ESV®), copyright © 2001 by Crossway, a publishing ministry of Good News Publishers. Used by permission. All rights reserved.

Scriptures marked ISV are taken from the *Holy Bible: International Standard Version®*. Copyright © 1996-forever by The ISV Foundation. ALL RIGHTS RESERVED INTERNATIONALLY. Used by permission.

The Jerusalem Bible. DARTON, LONGMAN and TODD Ltd. And Doubleday and Company. London. 1968.

The Holy Bible, New Living Translation, copyright ©1996, 2004, 2007 by Tyndale House Foundation. Used by permission of Tyndale House Publishers, Inc., Carol Stream, Illinois 60188. All rights reserved.

The Living Bible copyright © 1971 by Tyndale House Foundation. Used by permission of Tyndale House Publishers Inc., Carol Stream, Illinois 60188. All rights reserved.

New American Standard Bible®, Copyright © 1960, 1962, 1963, 1968, 1971, 1972, 1973, 1975, 1977, 1995 by The Lockman Foundation Used by permission."

(www.Lockman.org)

New King James Version®. Copyright © 1982 by Thomas Nelson, Inc. Used by permission. All rights reserved."

Weymouth New Testament in Modern Speech. Third Edition 1913. (Public Domain).

Contents

Chapter 1 – Benaiah: Overcoming Adversity.............. 15

Chapter 2 – Why Make Faith Confessions? 23

Chapter 3 – Sarah: God gives Abilities 31

Chapter 4 – Gideon: Overcoming the Odds............... 41

Chapter 5 – Joshua and Jonah: Overcoming the Enemy outside and within 53

Chapter 6 – John the Baptist: When God does not do what we want Him to do 65

Chapter 7 – Get Godly Wisdom and Make Good Decisions 71

Chapter 8 – 3 Kinds of Forgiveness 95

Chapter 9 – Faith.. 109

INTRODUCTION

This mini-book is one of four taken from my book "Lessons from my Dog: 33 Faith-Lifters to bless and build believers." Each mini-book is a topical collection of life-transforming and equipping messages that cover a variety of subjects.

These are Holy Spirit inspired revelations, Biblical teachings, testimonies and illustrations that have proven fruitful in the lives of many people during my years as Senior Pastor of a thriving Spirit-filled, Apostolic church and travelling prophetic minister.

They will help you develop your God-given potential in Christ and equip you to fulfil your ministry that the Lord has assigned to you, by doing the good works of love and faith that He prepared in advance for you to do. (Ephesians 2:10).

I am honoured by the affirming comments of my anointed, experienced and internationally significant endorsers. Their reviews have confirmed to me that these books are going to meet needs, change lives, multiply ministry, equip believers and fulfil the purposes that the Lord entrusted to me when He anointed me as an author.

1. Benaiah: *Overcoming Adversity*

³⁵ So do not throw away your confidence; it will be richly rewarded. ³⁶ You need to persevere so that when you have done the will of God, you will receive what He has promised.

Hebrews 10:35-36

Benaiah was one of David's best warriors. A local village was being terrorised by a marauding lion. They asked Benaiah to help kill the beast.

On the day arranged, when he woke up, Benaiah realised that it was a bitterly cold day. So, he decided to stay in bed and he never helped the villagers.

That is not true.

He thought: "Those people need me, so off I go."

As he walked toward the village, it started snowing. So, Benaiah turned around and went home to the cosy open fire in his living room.

That is not true.

He thought: "More people will die or be seriously injured if I turn back. So, onward I go."

When he got close to the village, Benaiah fell into a lion trap which the villagers had dug. They had covered the pit with leaves and branches, which were now disguised even further by a light covering of snow.

Benaiah thought: "I knew this was not the Lord's Will for me to stick my nose into other people's business. It was just my idea to come. God has been trying to tell me all the time that I shouldn't be going on this mission."

That is not true.

Benaiah would have thought. "Lord, this is Your mission. You have made me a defender of Your people. So, this is my God-given mission and I expect You to help me overcome all obstacles to make these, Your people, safe."

After some time, during which Benaiah was praying, praising, exercising, practicing his skills in warfare and digging some handholds and footholds in the wall of the pit, the lion dropped into the very same pit.

Benaiah thought: "Oh no, here we go again. My day has gone from bad to worse. Now I'm trapped in a pit with this big, hungry beast, who is going to have me for lunch. I wish I had stayed home. I really must be out of the Will of God, even though all this time I thought I was doing His Will."

Of course he didn't think like that.

Rather, Benaiah thought: "Praise God, You have answered my prayers and I give You glory because You care for Your people so much that You have delivered this lion into my hands." Then he would have said to the lion, something like David said to Goliath in 1 Samuel 17:45-47: "Lion, you are going down right now, in the Name of the Lord."

That is why the Bible says in 1 Chronicles 11:22 that Benaiah "went down into a pit on a snowy day and killed a lion."

What about you?

What does it take for you to have a bad day?

What does it take to divert you from your life's purpose?

How much do you trust the Lord's covenant partnership with you when times get tough?

Do you believe that God plus one, namely you, is a majority?

Do you believe that through faith in God, you can overcome not just one adverse thing, but a whole series of adverse events?

If God be for you, who or what can be successful against you?

One of the great lessons the Lord has taught me is this: persistence overcomes enemy resistance. In fact, persistence overcomes all resistance.

Persistence overcomes all resistance

The corollary to this is that God is faithful to us in all seasons and situations.

If one thing goes wrong (it's bitterly cold), don't think God has left you or you are out of His Will.

If another thing goes wrong (it starts snowing), don't think God has left you or you are out of His Will.

If something else goes wrong (you fall into a pit), don't think God has left you or you are out of His Will.

If even a fourth or fifth or sixth thing goes wrong (such as a hungry lion dropping in for lunch unannounced), don't think God has left you or you are out of His Will.

God is always faithful.

However, you have to make sure that you are living in His Will, which means according to His Word; and make sure you learn how to hear the Voice of God on a personal and lifestyle basis, so that you are indeed being led by His Spirit.

The wonderful thing about the day of grace in which we live is that God is faithful, even when we are not (2 Timothy 2:13); but, don't become presumptuous about that. Don't put God to the test. (Matthew 4:7).

Of course, my story is not told in the Bible. There is just a one-sentence summary of what happened. So, I want to expand the illustration by imagining that Benaiah had four friends who agreed to come with him on this dangerous mission.

One of them, Levi, didn't turn up on the morning because it was too cold. Another, Nahshon, got cold feet just as they were about to leave but covered up his feelings of fear and inconvenience by saying he would stay home and safeguard the people of Benaiah's village.

A third, Jesher, gave up the cause when it started snowing. He said he was concerned that it might crush his tent and he had better get home to protect his family.

How do you react when your supporters turn back? Does it influence you to quit? Are you like Jesus Who set His face like a flint to fulfil His Father's purpose, no matter how many scattered, no matter who betrayed him?

Benaiah's fourth friend lasted all the way until he heard the lion's roar and Benaiah fell into the pit. Hezron said: "I'll go for help"; but Benaiah did not see him again that day. He went the long way back to Benaiah's village, rather than the short way to reach the endangered villagers, because he was afraid to go any closer to that hungry, roaring lion.

Let me ask you: Is your faith strong enough to stand the test of people letting you down? Are you like the old song: "I have decided to follow Jesus, no turning back, no turning back. Though none go with me, yet still I'll follow, no turning back, no turning back?"

What is one thing you have learned from this teaching?

_____

What is one thing you can do to implement this teaching?

_____

Faith Declaration:

I thank You Lord for Your covenant partnership in my life. I declare that in Christ I can, and by faith I will, do all the things I need to do in order to live a satisfying, successful and un-selfish life. I praise You, Lord because I can be strong in You, even when I feel weak or people around me are weak, because Christ in me strengthens me. I declare in Jesus' Name that Your faithfulness will sustain me and Your Spirit empower me to stay the course, to fulfil my mission and to win the victory, because my battles are Your battles and victory belongs to the Lord. Amen.

Overcoming: Faith Food Snack Pack

2 Why Make **Faith Confessions?**

It is written: "I believed; therefore I have spoken." Since we have that same spirit of faith, we also believe and therefore speak
2 Corinthians 4:13

We all know, from both good and bad experiences, that words can heal, help or hurt. The important thing to understand is that your words can not only heal, help or hurt your listeners, but yourself as well, because you also hear what you say. We cannot control what other people say, but every Christian must learn how to take control of his own mind, moods and mouth.

"The tongue has the power of life and death,..."
Proverbs 18:21a

[12] Whoever of you loves life and desires to see many good days, [13] keep your tongue from evil and your lips from speaking lies.
Psalm 34:12-13

The Hebrew word for "evil" used by the Psalmist has these various meanings; through them, the Lord is telling us what kinds of words to not speak: bad, disagreeable, malignant; unpleasant, causing pain, unhappiness, misery; evil, displeasing; of low value; sad, unhappy; unkind, vicious in disposition or temper; ethically bad, wicked. So, if you want to love your life and see many good days, learn to not use words that fit into any of those negative categories.

Your words have power and they can do both harm and good. God wants you to use them for good, but the devil wants you to use them for harm. Believers who build enjoyable relationships and enduring ministries harness the positive power of their tongue.

What we speak is a matter of choice. God wants us to choose to speak for His glory and for the blessing and benefit of people. He wants us to reject being the mouthpiece of the devil or this world.

> *[10] And so blessing and cursing come pouring out of the same mouth. Surely, my brothers and sisters, this is not right! [11] Does a spring of water bubble out with both fresh water and bitter water?*
>
> *James 3:10-11*

Why Make Faith Confessions?

Our words must be like living water perfumed with grace, not bitter water laced with acid.

One thing you can be sure of is that you will reap the consequences of how you choose to use your tongue.

> *From the fruit of his lips a man is filled with good things as surely as the work of his hands rewards him.*
>
> *Proverbs 12:14*

Just as your hands or work ethic can lead you to prosperity or poverty, so will the words of your mouth affect the quality of your life.

If you are a person who speaks positively, people will be attracted to you. Having a fault-finding, blame-shifting and critical tongue will ruin the quality of your life and relationships. It will also sabotage not only your own potential and destiny, but also that of any other people who are damaged by your negative words.

I have included this chapter (a) to remind you of how powerful your words are; and (b) to explain why the faith confessions I have included in every chapter are an important way for you to gain positive outcomes by activating the principles God has given me to share with you in this book.

I challenge you:

(i) to go on a thirty-day verbal fast from negativity;
(ii) to speak only that which encourages and blesses yourself and others during that time; and,
(iii) to say out loud, in a personalised way, the promises of God on a regular basis, for the rest of your life. You personalise the Scriptures, for example, by changing the "he" to "me" or inserting your name into the verse.

If you want to grow in faith and see the blessings and miracles you are believing for, you simply must come into agreement with what God's Word says to you and about you.

If you do not agree with God and His Word, then you will not receive what He has freely and already (past tense) given you in Christ. You can literally talk yourself out of your blessing. You can talk yourself out of your miracle; or, you can choose to talk yourself into your blessing, you can choose to talk yourself into your miracle, as the Bible teaches you to do. It's your choice and you will reap the result of that choice, positively or negatively.

The words we say are an expression of our faith. Speaking is one of the ways by which we put our faith in action. When we speak out what God's Word

Why Make Faith Confessions?

says about our mind, body, finances, relationships, circumstances, ministry and future it brings us into partnership with God, because we are in alignment with His Will for us. (1 John 5:14-15).

We all know that creation did not happen until God spoke it into being (as in Genesis chapter 1). It is important to realise that Holy Spirit was hovering over the earth, but nothing happened until God spoke.

This is also true for many Christians. Holy Spirit is hovering over their lives but nothing miraculous is happening because they are not speaking God's Word over their own lives. Speaking God's Word over your life is what turns Holy Spirit atmosphere into Holy Spirit action.

This principle is taught in both the Old and New Testaments. God Himself initiated it.

> [22] *The LORD said to Moses,* [23] *"Tell Aaron and his sons, 'This is how you are to bless the Israelites. Say to them:* [24] *"The LORD bless you and keep you;* [25] *the LORD make his face shine on you and be gracious to you;* [26] *the LORD turn his face toward you and give you peace."* [27] *"So they will put My Name on the Israelites, and I will bless them. Numbers 6:22-27*

Notice the word "how" in verse 23. The Lord was teaching them a method by which, if they implemented it, they would be blessed. The method involved a two-part process.

First, the priest had to speak the words of blessing over the people. The effect of this was to spiritually brand the people of God. This is the meaning of "put My Name on" them in verse 27. The second part was that the Lord would see all the people who had been spiritually branded by the words that were spoken over them and then He would bless them (verse 27) in accordance with what had been spoken.

Numbers 6:22-27 says, in effect: you, the Lord's New Testament priest (1 Peter 2:5 and 9), say it and God will do it.

When you speak the Word of God over your life, you spiritually brand yourself. The Lord sees what is branded on you by His Word and He will do it.

This concept of being spiritually branded for blessing is referred to by Paul in Ephesians 1:13-14. He tells his readers that after they first believe, they are secondly "marked in Him" (NIV) with Holy Spirit as their Divine Guarantee, by Whom and through

Why Make Faith Confessions?

faith, they will receive their inheritance, which is both in this life and throughout eternity.

The key thing to remember is that if the words are not spoken by faith and received by faith, the spiritual brand does not stick and the blessing won't be received.

What is one thing you have learned from this teaching?

_____

What is one thing you can do to implement this teaching?

_____

Faith Declarations:

- The Lord is my Shepherd I shall not want (Psalm 23:1)
- I can do all things through Christ Who strengthens me (Philippians 4:13)
- Through Jesus, I am adopted into the Father's Royal Family as a fully and personally loved son/daughter of God, who is worthy to receive all of God's blessings (Galatians 4:5-7)
- Through Jesus, I am made the righteousness of God in Christ. (2 Corinthians 5:21). The prayers of a righteous person are powerful & effective. (James 5:16). My prayers are powerful and effective.

3 Sarah:
God gives abilities

> *¹¹ By faith Sarah, even though she was old and barren, received the strength to conceive, because she was convinced that the One Who had made the promise was faithful.*
>
> *Hebrews 11.11 ISV*

> *⁴ Such confidence we have through Christ before God. ⁵ Not that we are competent in ourselves to claim anything for ourselves, but our competence comes from God. ⁶ He has made us competent as ministers of a new covenant*
>
> *2 Corinthians 3:4-6*

The Sydney celebration of the new millennium included a dazzling fireworks display centred on the iconic Sydney Harbour Bridge. During the celebration, the word "Eternity" was displayed on the bridge. This was because of a well-known piece of Sydney history.

For 24 years the identity of the person who wrote the word "Eternity" in a beautiful copperplate script on the pavements of Sydney streets was a matter of public interest. Then one Sunday a Baptist minister caught a man in his congregation, Arthur Stace, in the act of writing his one word Gospel on a Sydney street. The mystery was solved. The identity of the sidewalk preacher was revealed. The curiosity of the public and the media was satisfied.

The amazing thing was that Stace was uneducated. He couldn't read. For much of his life, Arthur was a drunken, petty criminal, who spent years in jail spread over several occasions.

He got saved and heard a preacher, John Ridley MC, say: "I wish I could sound or shout (the word "eternity") to everyone in the streets of Sydney." Immediately Stace felt a powerful calling from God to be the person who would make the word "eternity", and the God of eternity, famous in Sydney.

According to a brochure prepared by J. R. Ecob for The Herald of Hope Inc. in January 2000, Stace left church that morning and bent down to begin his decades long ministry of around 33 years, in which he wrote "eternity" more than 500,000 times.

Stace said: "The funny thing is that, before I wrote it, I could hardly spell my own name. I had no schooling and I couldn't have spelled "eternity" for a hundred quid *(Note: a "quid" was an Australian pound. Today's equivalent would be around $8,000).* But it came out smoothly, in a beautiful copperplate script. I couldn't understand it, and I still can't."

Arthur Stace is a fine example of God giving an ability to someone that they did not have. He demonstrates that the Lord empowers His people to do His work and will.

We love reading the miracles of Jesus where people received abilities they either never had or had lost; miracles, such as the blind having their sight restored, or the lame walking.

Ihor Lakatosh is a young Ukrainian boy who was so badly burned that one arm was fused to his body and he could not walk. His mother could not take care of him and so she decided to abandon him. His injuries were untreated for years, until he was accepted as a sponsored patient at Shriners Hospital for Children in Boston. On 19 June, 2014, the Huffington Post reported his interpreter quoting Ihor as saying: "Thank you I can walk. Thank you I can walk. Thank you Lord, I can walk." They noted that after so much sorrow in his life, Ihor now has a wonderful smile and often makes the sign of the cross as he is telling people his story of a life restored.

That is what Sarah, wife of Abraham, experienced. I believe her testimony is told in Hebrews 11:11, as written in the above ISV version. Some other versions give the credit here to Abraham, but his story is told in other places in Scripture.

Holy Spirit revealed to me that it was her story with this statement: "God gave her the ability to do something she couldn't do."

It is possible that Sarah did have the ability to bear children in her youth. If so, the Lord restored it.

God is ready, willing and able to do the same for you, in any and every area of your life, where you need a restored or new ability.

God is ready, willing and able to give you an ability you do not have, or an ability you have lost, in any and every area of life. You need to believe Him and His Word as Sarah did.

Sarah was not able to bear children. God renewed her youth, as well as Abraham's. Then she was able to carry and birth their child of promise, Isaac.

She came to the same place of fully-persuaded faith that Abraham did. (Romans 4:21). She became convinced that God meant what He said and said what He meant.

When the devil tempted Adam and Eve in the Garden, he attacked God's Word and then God's character. They fell for these two deceptions and paid a great price for their disobedience, a price all humanity has also been paying ever since.

Like Sarah, we have to come to the place of trusting God's Word and God's character, no matter how long we have been waiting for our miracle, no matter how unlikely it is to happen.

When we have this kind of fully-persuaded, convinced faith in both God's character and Word, He will give us abilities we didn't have, so we can do what we couldn't do before. Miracles will be normal for us, as they were for the apostle Peter. In Acts 3:12, after the amazing miracle of the healing of a man crippled from birth, Peter says to the assembled crowd: "Why does this surprise you?"

For centuries God has made apostles, prophets, evangelists, pastors and teachers out of farmers, housewives, fishermen, tax collectors, prisoners and whomever else He calls. The Lord has made millionaires out of what we call in Australia today "blue-collar workers." This demonstrates the well-known saying: "God doesn't call the qualified; He qualifies the called."

Holy Spirit can make you competent in any and every area of life and ministry. Yes, you will need to grow your faith. Yes, you will have to put your faith into action. Yes, you will have to renew your mind and harness your tongue. Yes, you might have to upskill yourself in the Word, the things of the Spirit, and even natural areas of knowledge and ability. When you do whatever you need to do, as Sarah did, Holy Spirit will help you step into greater levels of natural and supernatural abilities.

Recently, I read an interesting perspective on spiritual gifts, in regard to 1 Corinthians 12:11. The traditional way of understanding this verse is that Holy Spirit gives whatever gifts He decides to people. The Bible teacher I read is the first I have found in more than 38 years of Pentecostal Christianity to say that the Greek construction of the verse allows for a different translation. It can also be translated that Holy Spirit gives spiritual gifts just as the receiver determines. This is certainly in harmony with the two verses (1 Corinthians 12:31a & 14:1) that tell us we must earnestly desire spiritual gifts, especially that we might prophesy. Why would we be told to earnestly desire specific gifts, if Holy Spirit was intending to give us different ones? Selah!

When you look at the life of King David, you will see the progressive impartation of Divine abilities through the three anointings in his life.

The first, imparted by the prophet Samuel, to signal his future ministry of kingship enabled him to be a shepherd who could kill lions, bears and giants, because Holy Spirit came upon him mightily from that day forward. The anointing produced leadership and ministry capabilities in David that were not limited to his human abilities. David was empowered to be a prophetic worshipper, whose playing attracted the Presence of God so much that it caused demons to flee from King Saul. Previously, David had been a shepherd and a worshipper; but now the anointing brought the supernatural dimension of God's abilities into his life.

The anointing empowered him to prophesy defeat to Goliath, to kill that giant and then to lead Israel's army to victory over the Philistines. His abiding anointing was sufficient for him to lead his own small army for years. David started with four hundred men, who were in distress or in debt or discontented, at Adullam. (1 Samuel 22:2). The anointing on David's life helped him to turn them into an army of giant-killers.

David's second anointing was imparted by the tribe of Judah. (2 Samuel 2:4a). This anointing increased David's leadership ability to handle more than 500,000 men of military age. (This is according to the census in 2 Samuel 24:9). In other words, David's abilities went to another level for seven and a half years.

In 2 Samuel 5:3-4, David was anointed for the third and final time. He was anointed king over all Israel. This meant that an extra 800,000 men came under David's command. He now had 1.3 million men of military age to lead. The anointing of Holy Spirit increased his abilities to another level, again. He ruled for forty years.

David's life, leadership and ministry demonstrate that the greater the anointing, the greater the capacity of the one who has been anointed.

What is one thing you have learned from this teaching?

_____

What is one thing you can do to implement this teaching?

_____

Faith Declaration:

Thank You Lord that it's not by my might and it's not by my power, but it's by Your Spirit that mountains, blockages, problems and limitations will be removed from my life. I praise You that I can do all things through Christ Who strengthens me. I put my trust in You to help me walk and not faint, run and not grow weary, and rise up with wings like eagles. I thank You that from today I am receiving new and greater abilities, talents, anointings and spiritual gifts to do what I could not do before. By faith I declare that Holy Spirit is enlightening and empowering me to succeed in greater ways than ever before, in every area of my life, relationships and ministry, in Jesus' Name. Amen.

4   Gideon:
Overcoming the Odds

For God did not give us a spirit of timidity ..... but [He has given us a spirit] of power and of love and of a calm and well-balanced mind and discipline and self-control.

2 Timothy 1:7 AMP

The LORD turned to him and said, "Go in the strength you have and save Israel out of Midian's hand. Am I not sending you?"

Judges 6:14

In this chapter, I will show you six steps Gideon had to undertake in order to change his own life and the destiny of his family and nation.

(i)   Gideon had to change his self-perspective to agree with God.

It must have been an amazing thing for fearful Gideon to be visited by an angel. It was doubly amazing when the angel said that in God's opinion fraidy-cat Gideon was a mighty man of valour.

Gideon probably checked his temperature to make sure he didn't have a fever that was causing him to hallucinate. I guess that's why the Lord arranged for fire to supernaturally rise from the rock and consume the meat and bread that Gideon had offered Him as hospitality. You'd think the appearance and message of an angel would have been proof enough that God was speaking to him.

There are two things to note from the Lord's prophetic statement that referred to Gideon as a "mighty man of valour." Firstly, God doesn't put us down or use prophecy to point out our problems and weaknesses; rather, He speaks to our potential, knowing that His Word will kick-start a process of development in our lives. Secondly, take note of the word "process" I used. Gideon had a lot of changing and growing to do, before he actually became the mighty man of valour that the Lord had spoken into being over him.

The way the Lord did this was not to just flick His Divine fingers and shoo the spirit of fear out of Gideon. God gave Gideon several opportunities to face his fears and triumph over them. That's what He expects of every Christ-follower.

(ii)   Gideon had to overcome himself and his inner negatives.

One of the ways Gideon did that was in obedience to the Lord's command to: "Go in the strength that you have." (Judges 6:14). This is one of the most important principles of faith in the entire Bible. Gideon had to stop focussing on what he didn't have and use what he did have. When he did, Gideon proved that God was with him, rewarding his faith by giving him victory, success and prosperity.

(iii)   Gideon had to pull down his father's idol.

I wrote about this in my first book "You Can Prophesy – Supernatural. Simple. Safe."

Gideon's destruction of the altar of Baal is another example of prophetic action (Judges 6:25-27). Gideon could not change things on earth and gain a great victory for his people, unless and until he first got rid of the enemy's stronghold of idolatry, deception, theft, intimidation and bondage over the people of God.

I want you to notice the prophetic significance of God commanding Gideon to use the second bull. Normally the Lord always has the first and best offering. However, the second bull was seven years old, the exact age of the enemy's domination of Israel (Judges 6:1). So the sacrificial death of the seven year old bull was a prophecy of the end of the defeat and poverty God's people had experienced during the bull's lifetime. It was prophetic of the end of the enemy's domination of them.

Gideon's destruction of the pagan altar was prophetic of the breaking of demonic power over the people, and, after that spiritual victory, his courageous leadership brought about the freedom and prosperity of the entire nation for an entire generation of forty years. (Judges 8:28).

Gideon had to obey God even though he knew people would be angry with him – seriously, even dangerously, angry with him. That's a real challenge for a lot of people. But that's what it takes to be a believer. We have to do things God's way, even if we suffer for it. Sure enough, an argument broke out after Gideon tore down the idol; but his dad, Joash, quickly quenched it.

That quick victory was itself prophetic of other victories to come, because the enemy had now been stripped of the demonic spiritual power that had been aiding and abetting his evil cause.

(iv)   Gideon had to learn how to yield to Holy Spirit and desire His fullness.

Holy Spirit came upon Gideon to call the tribes to war against the massive invading army. The literal

Hebrew expression used in Judges 6:34 is that Holy Spirit clothed Himself with Gideon. How awesome is that. But it's not as awesome as what we New Testament believers have, which is the indwelling Presence of Holy Spirit

In the Old Testament, Holy Spirit came upon certain people at different times for specific purposes. In the New Testament, He is with each and every believer, all the time, for every good and godly purpose. Hallelujah.

As you look at this piece of history, you can see how Gideon was emboldened to blow the war trumpet by Holy Spirit "clothing" him.

Even with Holy Spirit's empowerment, Gideon still had to function in faith.

When, as many would describe it today, the anointing lifted, Gideon's fear got the better of him again. I don't blame him for that, because Israel was well and truly outnumbered by a combined army that had defeated them many times before.

So, Gideon puts out his two famous fleeces and in His grace and mercy, the Lord answers from Heaven to reassure Gideon of victory.

I love this Scripture:

> *For he (God) knows how weak we are; He remembers we are only dust.*
> *Psalm 103:14*

The Lord will help each and every one of us every step of the way. He is not fazed by the weakness of our humanity. However, God requires us to put our faith on the line in active partnership with Him, as Gideon did time and again.

(v) Gideon has to learn that faith is not a one-off act, but a lifestyle of obedience and taking risks for and with God.

So, Gideon has to reduce the size of his army, not once, but twice. This is military madness. If they were clearly outnumbered before, now the odds of 300 men defeating an army as thick as a locust plague, with too many camels to count, are beyond ridiculous. (Judges 7:12).

To his credit, Gideon did as the Lord had instructed him. If he had not, he would have disappeared from the pages of the Bible and God would have empowered another who would obey Him.

Now comes the most nonsensical challenge anybody could give a man, except for trained commandos, in the military situation Gideon now faced.

> That night the LORD said, "Get up! Go down into the Midianite camp, for I have given you victory over them! *10* But if you are afraid to attack, go down to the camp with your servant Purah. *11* Listen to what the Midianites are saying, and you will be greatly encouraged. Then you will be eager to attack." So Gideon took Purah and went down to the edge of the enemy camp.
>
> Judges 7:9-11 NLT

The Lord says to Gideon: "if you are afraid, go down to the (enemy) camp". Wouldn't it be better if God had said: "If you are afraid, retreat a few kilometres until the time is right to attack them"? or, "If you are afraid, I will show you the 100,000 angels I have accompanying you"?

Again, Gideon demonstrates how he got control over his negative feelings and probably eradicated them completely from his life.

He subdued them by confronting them and acting in faith by doing the very opposite of what his inner negatives were pressuring him to do. This demonstrates the familiar saying: "Faith and courage are not what we do in the absence of fear, but doing the right thing despite the fear."

Gideon controlled, subdued and eradicated his negative feelings by acting in faith

It was through the history of Gideon that the Lord first showed me this principle: Every situation of fear is also an opportunity for faith.

Every situation of fear is also an opportunity for faith

When Gideon arrived at the enemy camp, where there must have been literally thousands of tents, he crept up to the very one where he can overhear the men inside. At that very moment, one is describing a divine dream, with a meaning that frightens the enemy and encourages Gideon.

What are the odds of Gideon being in exactly the right place at exactly the right time? That's what God can do for you when you are on His side and He is on yours.

(vi)   Gideon has to learn that victory comes from attacking the enemy, not avoiding conflict.

Many have said: offence is the best form of defence. The Bible teaches that advancing the Kingdom of Heaven requires "violence", which means boldness and assertive, proactive faith. (Matthew 12:11).

Gideon's final test is to start the attack, by faith, using a God-given strategy and then complete the fight, until the enemy was so destroyed that they were not successful against Israel for another forty years. Hallelujah.

Now what about you? Are you ready to progressively overcome your fears and other inner negatives? Are you ready to consistently put your faith on the line according to the Word of God and the leading of His Spirit in order to partner with God to fulfil your potential and destiny?

Every Christian must exercise active faith in their various circumstances, opportunities and challenges of life. We are not to just passively wait for God to fight our spiritual enemies and overcome our different obstacles for us.

> *Be strong, all you people of the land," declares the LORD, 'and work. For I am with you,'*
>
> *Haggai 2:4,5*

> *³ Strengthen the feeble hands, steady the knees that give way; ⁴ say to those with fearful hearts, "Be strong, do not fear*
> Isaiah 35:3,4a

When you do the best you can and trust God to do the rest, the Lord will surely do what you cannot do.

What is one thing you have learned from this teaching?

_____

What is one thing you can do to implement this teaching?

_____

Faith Declaration:

I thank You Lord for helping me grow by overcoming my fears and other negatives and inner hindrances. Thank You for enabling me to confront and be victorious over any giant or mountain or army that is in my way. I praise You because Your Divine Partnership empowers me to do far more than I could ever do alone. I exalt You as my Champion and Lord and thank You for enabling me to achieve victory, peace and prosperity in my life, for my family and my entire sphere of influence, in Jesus' Name. Amen.

Overcoming: Faith Food Snack Pack

5. Joshua and Jonah: Overcoming the Enemy Outside and Within

"The word of the Lord came to Jonah .... But Jonah ran away from the Lord ..."
Jonah 1:1 & 3

... Now then, you and all these people, get ready to cross the Jordan River into the land I am about to give to them — to the Israelites. [3] I will give you every place where you set your foot, as I promised Moses.... [5] No one will be able to stand against you as long as you live. For I will be with you as I was with Moses. I will not fail you or abandon you.

Joshua 1:2-3 & 5

Then the Lord said to Joshua, "See, I have delivered Jericho into your hands along with its king and its fighting men. ... [27] So the Lord was with Joshua, and his fame spread throughout the land.

Joshua 6:2 & 27

Some years ago I felt the Lord was prompting me to preach a series based on the book of Jonah. I wasn't keen on that idea. So, I did what I tell others not to do. I started asking around our church to see if I could find someone who would agree with me and give me an excuse to not preach about Jonah.

Perhaps I didn't sell my case very well. Starting with "I think God wants me to preach the book of Jonah" was probably not going to gain me many naysayers. Sure enough, pretty much the standard answer I got was: "Well, if the Lord is telling you to do it, you'd better go ahead and preach it." At least I discovered that I had taught the people to obey God.

Around this time, we had a serious church meeting of a select number of leaders. A staff member premeditatedly and without warning to me hijacked the meeting to attack me. It felt like he walked up to me with a knife in his hand and used it as Ehud did in Judges 3:19-21. It seemed like he twisted it and threw in as much salt as he could.

Somehow, on the outside, I maintained my equilibrium and got through the rest of the meeting, which you might easily surmise did not achieve any great or godly purpose.

As I drove away from the meeting, I thought "I am going to drive far out of town and stay out of contact for three days and three nights."

About fifty metres ahead of me was a set of traffic lights. I was intending to turn toward the highway and just keep on going. But in those few metres, Holy Spirit spoke to me. God said: "Be a Joshua, not a Jonah." In other words, don't run away as Jonah did. Stay here and win this battle. Don't be robbed of your (plural, meaning our whole church) Promised Land inheritance.

So, I went home and the next night, I repaired the damage done in a second meeting with all concerned.

Then Holy Spirit said: "Now, I want you to preach a series on Joshua, not Jonah." I did that and it was one of the best teaching series I ever did.

Holy Spirit said to me: Be a Joshua, not a Jonah

Can you see how the Lord knew in advance what was going to happen that negative night? Yet, He didn't save me from it. Rather, He prepared me to learn from it, grow through it and overcome it.

That's what He did with Gideon. God didn't click His fingers to take away Gideon's fears. The Lord gave him opportunities to confront his fears and overcome them by acting courageously. Gideon did so by developing a wonderful and powerful partnership with Holy Spirit. (Judges 6:34). I did the same.

Gideon won for his nation and family a generation of peace and prosperity. I and the people who teamed with me have built a lasting outpost of God's Kingdom in our area. Indeed, the people of our local church will send out the love, truth and power of God for generations to come.

I proved in those two nights, and on many other occasions when problems needed solving and miracles just had to happen, two well-known sayings: "Leadership is lonely"; and "God plus one is a majority."

If God is for us who can be against us?
Romans 8:31

When I was in high school, I had a strange way of getting to class. Instead of getting the bus that went left, in the direction of my school, I used to get an earlier bus that went right. That bus took me to a downtown stop where the girls from Smith Street Girls School used to catch their bus. One of those young ladies had caught my eye, big-time.

One day while at the bus stop with her, three guys, who were their own small gang, approached me. They threatened me by saying if they ever saw me with that girl again they would attack me.

It was not in my best interests to argue with them, when the odds were three against one. So, I enlisted the help of my two strong, athletic friends, Nick and Ziggy. A few days later, we approached the three young men, their faces dropped and their bravado left them.

Why? Because Nick, although not tall, was a very strong, athletic-looking teenager whose chest was almost as wide as the street on which we were walking and his biceps were as large as a grown man's thighs. Ziggy was so big and strong that when he walked down the street he blocked out the sun.

My three adversaries refused my invitation to settle the matter that afternoon. They accepted my peace terms unconditionally and never bothered me again.

I had realised that if I let this gang intimidate me, then I could never enjoy the freedom of getting to know that very interesting young lady and I would no longer have the freedom of my city that I enjoyed. I would have to avoid that part of town. Therefore, I acted in both faith and wisdom in order to maintain my quality of life.

The help I got from Nick and Ziggy that day is the merest fraction of the infinite help the Lord has committed Himself to giving me and every true child of His. Hallelujah! I have often illustrated the difference between God and the devil this way: God is a herd of elephants; the devil is an ant. That's sums up the level of support we have with the Lord being always on our side and by our side.

So it's as true as every other promise of God in His Word: If God is for us who or what can be against us?

The courage I got that day as a school student from having my two friends with me gives a small indication of how Joshua must have felt after he met the Lord as Commander-in-Chief of the Armies of God, meaning both angelic and Israelite on earth. (Joshua 5:13-15).

Joshua also drew courage from what the Lord had spoken to him in Joshua 1:1-9, which included the specific promise of the Lord's accompanying "Emmanuel – God with us" Presence.

> ... for the LORD your God will be with you wherever you go.
>
> Joshua 1:9

It is a powerful thing to have your faith built by the Word of the Lord. When that Word is added to by the manifest Presence of the Lord, faith soars to far greater heights. So, we must be people of both the Word and of the Presence, if we want to take nations for and with God.

Joshua did both of these. The commandment the Lord gave him, which if obeyed would ensure his ongoing prosperity and success, was to meditate on the Word of God day and night and obey it. (Joshua 1:7-8). In Exodus 33:11 we are told that Joshua loved the Presence of God. Even after Moses left the tent where the Glory cloud of God had manifested, Joshua would stay there.

Similarly, Christians must know the Word of God personally and not think they will grow strong in the Lord on an inconsistent diet of Sunday sermons. We also have to cultivate intimacy with the Lord on a daily, not weekly or fortnightly basis. This enables us to hear God's Voice and partner with Him. Thirdly, we must put our faith on the line in practical, active ways, in obedience to the Word and as the Lord leads.

The two words translated prosperity and success in Joshua 1:8 are interesting.

The Hebrew word for prosperity is "tsachal". It literally means to advance, prosper, rush, attack or breach. In other words, if you want to prosper, you are going to have to learn how to overcome opposition and adversity. You are going to have to "get on the front foot", as our cricketing friends say. You will have to be proactive in working for a prosperous life or business or ministry.

The second Hebrew word is "sakal", which literally means to act wisely. It is mentioned four times in regard to David's success in one chapter. (1 Samuel 18:5,14,15,30). Verse 14 says that David was so successful, more successful than anyone else, because the Lord was with him. This is the very same key to success attributed to Joseph in Genesis 39:3,21,23.

So, if you want to succeed in life, you need to ask God for His wisdom in your major decisions, and you must cultivate your personal friendship and partnership with the Lord. You cannot act like the village clown or like some crazy character on a mid-morning television soap opera and expect to be successful.

The two key principles I want you to get from this chapter are in the title.

Firstly, in order to be successful in life, you must overcome the enemy within.

To be successful, you must overcome the enemy within

Jonah really did not do this, as you can see for yourself by reading chapter 4 of his book in the Bible. So, he occupies only a small part of the Bible compared to what he could have done if he had sorted himself out on the inside.

Moses missed out on the Promised Land because he didn't get control of his anger problem. In chapter 6 of my first book "You Can Prophesy – Supernatural. Simple. Safe.", I wrote: "In Exodus 17:6, Moses struck the rock in order to produce a massive amount of water, enough to satisfy two and a half million people, enough to save them from physical death in the wilderness. This was prophetic of the fact that Jesus would be struck on Calvary, so that the world might be saved from spiritual death, in the spiritual wilderness of sin.

Moses was not allowed to enter the Promised Land because he wrote a prophetic mistake into the pages of God's book. When he struck the rock a second time, instead of speaking to it, as God had commanded him, Moses effectively wrote into the bible that Jesus would be struck twice, which He wasn't. (Numbers 20:7-12). Jesus' once-only sacrifice on Calvary was more-than-sufficient for the salvation of mankind, for their restoration to relationship and partnership with God, for the stripping of the devil of his authority as the god of this world. So, God told Moses, on the second occasion, to speak to the rock, because after Calvary, all we believers have to do is speak to the Lord and every blessing and resource we need, that has all been paid for by Jesus' sacrifice and triumph, is released to us through answered prayer."

When you read Numbers 20:10 today, centuries after it was written, you can still feel the frustration and anger in Moses' words.

Moses said to them, *"Listen, you rebels, must we bring you water out of this rock?"* (Numbers 20:10).

In verse 12, the Lord adds another sin to Moses' disobedience. As well as dishonouring God by saying must "we" (meaning himself and Aaron, not the Lord) bring you water, the Bible says Moses was acting in unbelief when he struck the rock. He just didn't believe that speaking to the rock would produce the same result as occurred when he struck the rock in the book of Exodus.

Secondly, as we see demonstrated in Joshua's many victories to take possession of the Promised Land, we must confront the external adversities and adversaries we are faced with in life and ministry.

To be successful requires us to confront and overcome our external adversities and adversaries

Your strategy to overcome must take into account these two factors: (a) that *"our struggle is not against flesh and blood"*. (Ephesians 6:12). We do not treat people in the ordinary course of our lives as our enemies; (b) the weapons we use to overcome both people and things, that are opposing our progress in line with the Will and purposes of God, are spiritual. Our weapons of succeeding over opposition and adversity are not military, nor are they the weapons the world teaches us to use against others, such as gossip and criticism. Our weapons are things such as prayer, love, faith and Godly wisdom.

What is one thing you have learned from this teaching?

_____

What is one thing you can do to implement this teaching?

_____

Faith Declaration:

I thank You Lord for helping me overcome my hurts and fears. I thank you that I am a Joshua, not a Jonah. I praise You for partnering with me to build a great life, family and ministry that is changing the world around me, one step and one day at a time. I declare that I will not be intimidated by people, circumstances or threats from the devil in my mind. I praise you because You have not given me a spirit of fear, but of power, love and a sound mind and self-control. Therefore, I decree that I will do all the things I need to do, in order to live a victorious, successful and prosperous life by faith and by the empowering of Your Holy Spirit.

6

John the Baptist:
When God does not do what we want Him to do

Blessed is anyone who does not stumble on account of Me.
Luke 7:23

But wisdom is proved right by all her children.
Luke 7:35

Some years ago, I was in the middle of a stressful ministry season. I did something I have done only once in more than thirty years of ministry. I called a pastor friend. I told him, I had no motivation to preach that Sunday and asked him to step in for me. Even though it was short notice, he did a great job for the Lord and our congregation.

I took off for the weekend with some teaching videos (remember them?). As I watched them over the next forty-eight hours, I got quite a kick in the rear end from the Lord.

Holy Spirit really spoke to me through John the Baptist's experience, as described in Luke 7:18-35. I realised I was upset not only with people and circumstances, but with the Lord Himself, because He wasn't doing what I wanted Him to do for me.

When John the Baptist was imprisoned, he wanted Jesus to rescue him. Who wouldn't?

John's frustrated expectations led him to doubt the supernatural revelation that God Himself had given him. He began to question whether Jesus really was the Messiah, even though he had received prophetic insight that Messiah was coming and a supernatural vision of Holy Spirit descending upon Jesus like a dove, when John baptised Him.

This is the same tactic the devil used in the Garden of Eden. He incited Adam and Eve to doubt God's Word and then God's character.

We are not true believers if we begin to doubt God's Word and/or character just because the Lord is not doing what we want Him to do. The quality of God's character and the truth of His Word is not dependent upon our needs or circumstances.

Jesus' message to the disciples of John was that they could tell John the proof of His Messiah-ship was that the Gospel was being preached with signs following.

It is significant that Jesus did not say anything about John's future, nor did He promise to go to the prison to visit or free John.

The first of two standout statements Jesus made that I needed to learn from was verse 23.

I had to learn to refuse to stumble in faith over things the Lord did or didn't do; or things the Lord said or didn't say; or things the Lord did for others but not for me.

John was actually, without him knowing it at the time, at the end of his ministry and near the end of his life. I think most of us would prefer to not know when that day was coming. I encourage you to pray as I do, that the Lord, by His grace, will enable you to finish well – relationally, with God and people, internally, ministerially, circumstantially, in health and in finances ... and in how and when you die.

Most of us are not in the place of nearness to death – but I gladly admit I am one of those Christians who believe that Jesus could come at any time. Therefore we should live as those who are ready to meet Him at any time.

Assuming we have a lot more life to live with and for the Lord, you need to learn, as I did, how to pass the test of both faith and character which John had to when he received Jesus' reply from his disciples.

He had to rejoice in the blessings and miracles that others were receiving from God, while at the same time not getting an answer about or a miracle for his own situation.

We have to learn to let God be God. Romans 12:15 tells us to "rejoice with those who rejoice and mourn with those who mourn". That is harder to do when others are rejoicing and you are mourning. A mature Christian grows to be able to do this.

I had to learn to refuse to stumble in faith over things the Lord did or didn't do; or things the Lord said or didn't say; or things the Lord did for others, but not for me.

The second verse that tested me and helped me grow at that time was verse 35. God is wise enough to do the right thing for every person in every situation. We must trust Him, at the same time recognising that His thoughts are not always the same as our thoughts and His ways are not always how we think He should act.

There is another principle I had to learn from John's experience, or more particularly from Jesus' silence in regard to John's personal situation: we must trust the character of God, no matter what. We must trust the Word of God and hold on to the revelation God has already given us, without the need for God to have to repeat Himself every time our faith gets shaky. The Lord does not have to keep telling us what we already know.

If there is a promise from God in His Word that fits our situation, then that is enough for us to believe for the miracle we need. God does not have to say or do any more. When we have faith in what God has already said and what Jesus has already done, we are ready for a miracle.

When we have faith in what God has already said and what Jesus has already done, we are ready for a miracle.

The only hitch is that we have to wait for the appointed time. That time will be when we have the faith equal to the answer we need. That is what happened to Abraham, as you can see in Romans 4:16-21. When he became "fully persuaded", his miracle came to pass. We are his faith-children. (Galatians 3:13-14, 29). We operate the same faith principles as Abraham did, but under a better covenant.

This same principle is found in Jesus' statement about receiving Holy Spirit. "If any man is thirsty, let him come to Me and drink. Whoever believes..." (John 7: 37-38). When you are thirsty, you are ready. Thirstiness signals God's time has come. Coming and drinking is belief; it is faith in action.

What is one thing you have learned from this teaching?

_____

What is one thing you can do to implement this teaching?

_____

Faith Declaration:

I thank You, Lord, that I can count on Your character, Word and wisdom, Your faithfulness, power and provision at all times in my life. I declare that I will trust You in good times and in tough times. I lean on Your Word and not my own understanding. I confess my faith in the promises of God and expect You to provide all I need to succeed, in Jesus' Name. Amen.

Overcoming: Faith Food Snack Pack

7

Get Godly Wisdom
and Make Good Decisions

The beginning of Wisdom is: get Wisdom (skillful and godly Wisdom)! [For skillful and godly Wisdom is the principal thing.] And with all you have gotten, get understanding (discernment, comprehension, and interpretation).

Proverbs 4:7 AMP

The King James version of this verse says: "*Wisdom is the principal thing.*"

The New Living Translation reads: *"Getting wisdom is the wisest thing you can do!"*

If you read Proverbs chapter 3, you will see the following benefits of having wisdom are listed:

(i) Extended lifespan with peace and prosperity;
(ii) The Lord will direct and make straight and plain your paths. Always let Him lead you, and He will clear the road for you to follow. Seek His will in all you do and He will show you which path to take;

(iii) Health to your body and nourishment to your bones;

(iv) Riches and honour;

(v) Pleasant ways, peace and blessing;

(vi) Safety and sweet sleep;

(vii) You will not be afraid of sudden disaster or ruin, for the LORD will be at your side and will keep your foot from being snared or stumbling.

Don't you want those benefits in your life? I'm sure you do, as I do. So, let's look at how we can increase in godly wisdom, which is defined in James 3:13-18.

7 Ways to get Godly Wisdom

(i) Cultivate the Fear of the Lord

Fear of the LORD is the foundation of wisdom. Knowledge of the Holy One results in good judgment...

Proverbs 9:10 NLT

The fool says in his heart, "There is no God."

Psalm 14:1

Wisdom starts when you fall in love with the Lord and choose a lifestyle of obeying God with a worshipful sense of adoration, awe, respect and submission.

A fool finds pleasure in doing mischief, wrong and evil conduct: but a man of

understanding delights in wisdom; living wisely brings pleasure to the sensible.
Proverbs 10:23

Cultivating the fear of the Lord in your life is not just a spiritual thing; it is a commitment to a relationship with the Lord and to a lifestyle that pleases Him. We love Father God because He is so perfect, so good and so beautiful. We also admire, worship and obey Him because He is our Creator, our Lord and, one day, our Judge and our Rewarder.

If you are wise and understand God's ways, prove it by living an honorable life, doing good works with the humility that comes from wisdom.

James 3:13 NLT

When you are a believer who truly fears God in a worshipful way, you seek the Lord's Presence, His Heart and Mind and Hand and His Image in your life.

When you are a believer who truly fears God, you seek first the Kingdom of God, His Rulership in your life and His Purposes for you and for the world around you. You do this out of love and gratitude, not out of obligation or religious pressure.

When you are a believer who truly fears God, you can ask God to give you His Wisdom and He will. (James 1: 5-8).

If you use His wisdom, if you practice what you preach, you will start reaping all the benefits Proverbs 3 talks about.

(ii)   Position yourself to gain Knowledge and Understanding

Wisdom is gained by knowing facts and learning how they fit together to produce good outcomes.

> *A wise person is hungry for knowledge: but the fool feeds on stupidity and rubbish.*
> *Proverbs 15:14*

We do learn from God's Word. This is why He wrote it. His Word is full of instruction and godly wisdom for every life decision, especially the decision to get to know Him.

We don't learn only from textbooks or educational courses, we also learn from people who have succeeded in life. Even some who have failed can at least tell us, or help us discover, how they went wrong and we can learn from that.

The greatest teacher most of us learn wisdom from is experience; our own and other people's.

> *Simpletons only learn the hard way, but the wise learn by listening.*
> *Proverbs 21:11 The Message*

So, what is "experience"? It's not just an event. Experience is more to do with the life impact of that event and the personal growth that impact produces in us.

American comedian Will Rogers is credited with saying: "Good judgment comes from experience, and a lot of that comes from bad judgment."

That's a good explanation of what I mean regarding the personal growth that life's events and consequences produce in us. An experienced person has learned from and grown up through the school of hard knocks. In the process he has left behind the mistakes and pains of the past but taken with him the wisdom he has gained from both good and bad events in his life.

Let me give you a humourous piece of wisdom from an anonymous source who said it is useful to employ when you make a mistake: "If at first you don't succeed, cover your tracks so no-one finds out." Its sister saying is: "If at first you don't succeed, find someone or something to blame." I quickly add the reassurance to my readers that I do not advocate these philosophies. I include them only for your enjoyment.

Here are three more quotes that are also attributed to Will Rogers:

If stupidity got us into this mess, then why can't it get us out?

Never miss a good chance to shut up.

Live in such a way that you would not be ashamed to sell your parrot to the town gossip.

(iii) Surround yourself with people who can provide you with good counsel, including correction.

Wise Christians are accountable to others. They seek personal life change, as well as the up-skilling of their abilities and spiritual gifts.

> *Fools think their own way is right; but the wise listen to the advice of others.*
>
> *Proverbs 12:15*
>
> *Plans go wrong for lack of advice; many advisers bring success.*
>
> *Proverbs 15:22 NLT*
>
> *Without consultation, plans are frustrated, but with many counselors they succeed.*
>
> *Proverbs 15:22 NAS*

(iv) Plan ahead

A prudent person foresees danger and takes precautions. The simpleton goes blindly on and suffers the consequences.

Proverbs 22:3 and 27.12 NLT

You have probably heard a saying similar to this: One teaspoon of prevention is better than a truckload of cure.

It happens to be true.

God Himself plans ahead. (Isaiah 25:1). Prophecy is a declaration of God's plan for the future. Jeremiah 29:11 tells us that He has good plans for us. The Lord has also planned, from even before we were born, what good works He intends for us to do in the life. God doesn't just act spontaneously. Jesus was born at the pre-arranged time, the appointed time or as Galatians 4:4 puts it in "the fullness of time".

When I was teaching at Wollongong University and the Gippsland Institute of Advanced Education, my students knew if I had prepared my lecture or tutorial or not. It was far more stressful for me to teach at that level if I went into the classroom unprepared and it was far less helpful to my students.

I know there are some ministers who can successfully preach spontaneously, and they might even say prophetically, on a regular basis. I can tell you that such preachers are few and far between and they are successful only because they are very knowledgeable of God's Word and very experienced in communicating His Truth. They have years of serious Bible study and of preparing messages behind them.

Too many people want to preach spontaneously and call it prophetic, because they are too lazy to prepare a decent meal for the people of God. They feed the Lord's people instant, ready-flavoured milk or someone else's revelation. I need to warn you that even when you are in the pulpit, under an anointing of Holy Spirit, you are not infallible. You can still say the wrong thing. It is more honouring to God, more beneficial to His people and safer for you, if you step up to speak with a prepared word from God. By all means let Holy Spirit tweak it while you are speaking, but don't presume that all you have to do to be a preacher is to open your mouth and He will fill it. That is twisting what the Psalmist (81:10) wrote to fit your own slackness.

(v) Control yourself

> God has not given us a spirit of fear, but of power, love and a sound mind, self-discipline and self-control
>
> 2 Timothy 1:7

What do you need to control in your life? Let me suggest a few specific areas: Your Mind, Emotions, Tongue, Sexuality, Stomach and your other appetites, Money, Actions and Reactions etc.

> People with understanding control their anger: but a quick- and hot-tempered man shows great foolishness.
>
> Proverbs 14:29 (also 12.16 and 29.11)

Let me give you two pieces of advice here:

Firstly, when something goes wrong or someone says something you do not like, take a deep breath, take some time to calm down and then respond to it. Don't react and, even more importantly, don't over-react to it. Pour water on the fire, not petrol.

Secondly, don't panic; stick to the game plan. As a Christian, that means sticking to God's game plan, which is the Word of God.

There are two Proverbs that the Lord has highlighted to me on a number of occasions over the years.

> *A person without self-control is like a city with broken-down walls.*
> *Proverbs 25:28 NLT*

A person who can't control himself, his tongue, his actions or reactions is vulnerable. He is easily overwhelmed by an enemy or out-manoeuvred by an opponent or manipulated by people.

I said a person who "can't" control himself, but I really meant "won't" control himself, because the Lord gives us self-control. So, saying you can't control yourself is a cop-out. You need to take responsibility for yourself. Then, you are more likely to act wisely and be victorious, prosperous and successful. You are more likely to gain the benefits of wisdom, because self-control is a sign of a mature and wise person.

> *Better a patient man than a warrior, a man who controls his temper than one who takes a city.*
> *Proverbs 16:32*

This verse tells us that the Lord ranks the development of our character higher than our achievements. So, developing Christ-like qualities such as self-control and wisdom will bring greater reward on that day when you stand before God.

(vi) Build good relationships and communication.

Learn how to and put the effort into being a good family member and a great team member or leader in every sphere of life and ministry.

> *He who walks with the wise grows wise: but a companion of fools gets into trouble and suffers harm.*
>
> *Proverbs 13:20*

> *Two people are better off than one, for they can help each other succeed.*
>
> *Ecclesiastes 4:9*

> *To answer before listening — that is folly and shame.*
>
> *Proverbs 18:13*

> *Don't use foul or abusive language. Let everything you say be good and helpful, so that your words will be an encouragement to those who hear them.*
>
> *Ephesians 4:29 NLT*

You need to develop good people and communication skills.

Some of these are:

(a) ability to encourage, empathise with, support, motivate and influence others

(b) building team identity, focus and action

(c) problem solving and conflict resolution

(d) listening

(e) understanding the importance of body language and tone of voice in communication;

(f) speaking confidently and clearly;

(g) talking to people and treating them in a friendly and respectful way;

(h) showing interest and compassion

(i) asking questions and letting people know that you believe what they have told you

(j) keeping an open mind, not jumping to false conclusions or making foolish assumptions –

remember: "to assume can make an ass out of you or me"

(k) honesty, integrity, reliability, including following through on your promises;

(l) exercising good and fair judgement in regard to both people and things

(m) having a sense of humour. Generally speaking, smiling creates a great atmosphere for communication, whether in casting vision, setting out policy directives, negotiating or problem solving. Of course there are occasions when a smile or humour can be quite inappropriate and counter-productive

(n) training, trusting and being patient with people.

(vii) Be a good and generous manager and investor of the money and of the true riches that the Lord entrusts to you.

> *There is treasure to be desired and oil in the dwelling of the wise; but a foolish man wastefully spends all he has.*
>
> *Proverbs 21:20*
>
> *And he who had received the five talents came forward, bringing five talents more, saying, Master, you delivered to me five talents;*

> here I have made five talents more.' ²¹ His master said to him, 'Well done, good and faithful servant. You have been faithful over a little; I will set you over much. Enter into the joy of your master.'
>
> Matthew 25:20-21 ESV

Those words of Jesus: "*Well done, good and faithful servant*" are not automatically heard by every Christian when they go to Heaven. To hear them you must "do" good things ("well") with the resources of time, talents, treasure, testimonies, truth and spiritual gifts that the Lord gives you. You must be a "good" person and a "good" servant who is "faithful" to God and His Word and His Will both in terms of (a) reliable, consistent, persistent friendship and partnership with the Lord over the long haul; and (b) demonstrating a lifestyle of active faith, which is being "faith-full".

12 Ways to make Wise, Godly, Good Decisions

It's not enough to get wisdom. You actually have to use it. Sadly King Solomon, who is often credited with being the wisest man who ever lived, did not take his own advice. Many people make that same mistake.

Get Godly wisdom and make good decisions

If Solomon is the author of Ecclesiastes, you can see how disillusioned he became. He also disobeyed his own wisdom and the Lord's commands by taking foreign wives and allowing them to continue their idolatrous practices. He did not finish well as he should have.

Decisions are the big and small blocks on which lives, ministries, businesses and organisations are built. There are all kinds of decisions we have to make each day, ranging from the unimportant to the urgent and to the significant. In this chapter I am talking about serious decisions, the kind that make a difference in your life. Some of these decisions do not seem life-changing straight away, but over time they can surely make or break you.

The first drink you take doesn't seem to hurt much. However if you get drunk, you can get into huge trouble. If you become an alcoholic, your life will really fall apart on so many levels, such as your health, relationships, employment and finances. This illustrates the fact that if you consistently make wrong decisions, your life can go really haywire. Sadly, sometimes just one bad decision can have huge negative long-term consequences.

Most of us have heard the saying: "*Everything happens for a reason.*" The thing is that sometimes the reason is that the person has not acted in godly wisdom, but in worldly stupidity. Don't blame the results of bad judgments, foolish choices or wrong decisions on fate or karma (I don't believe in either of those concepts) or the devil (although he could have inspired the negative situation) or, worst of all, on God (Who never does anything wrong, unfair or foolish). If you think God is your problem, then you won't have faith for Him to be your solution.

Making right decisions builds your character, relationships and future. The best decisions that produce the most favourable results are those that are Biblical and Spirit-led.

> *He who deals wisely and heeds [God's] word and counsel shall find good, and whoever leans on, trusts in, and is confident in the Lord — happy, blessed, and fortunate is he.*
>
> *Proverbs 16:20 AMP*

(i)   Have right motives, including wanting God's Will above all else.

(ii)   Read your Bible to discern God's Will and to make sure your decision is scripturally wise and valid. Two biblical principles you can check your decisions against are these: will it glorify God and will it do good for others?

Get Godly wisdom and make good decisions

(iii) Get your mind and emotions under the control of Holy Spirit. Don't make decisions in a state of turmoil or in the heat of the moment when you are reacting to something that has happened.

(iv) Pray to and listen to the Lord. As you pray, you will realise that what is of God will grow stronger, more attractive and more exciting to your faith. What is not of God will get weaker and become less appealing. As you pray, ask for God's wisdom. (James 1:5-8).

(v) Ask yourself: What would be the common sense decision? What have you learned from your training, from past experience and from things you have seen happen in other people's lives? Think about what advice you would give someone else in the same situation.

(vi) Make sure that what you are deciding is morally, ethically and legally acceptable.

(vii) Listen to wise, godly people, especially your own family and pastor or church group leader. Recently, at a family dinner, I casually raised the subject of me buying a small motor bike. The whole family with one voice howled me down. So, that means no motor bike for me. Let me tell you another great wisdom principle: "Happy wife, happy life."

(viii) Check your inner feelings.

- Do you have peace within? (Colossians 3:15).
- Is your faith, excitement and joy rising or falling?
- Do you feel any inner negatives? Are you getting cold inside about the matter under consideration?
- Even if you have some fear that may not necessarily mean it is the wrong thing to decide or be involved with; it may indicate you are nervous about your ability to succeed. That's when you need faith.
- You will have faith if and when you are confident that what you are making decisions about is God's Will for your life.

(ix) Is it in line with your life's purpose and giftedness?

(x) Is the timing right? Bishop Bill Hamon teaches that three things have to come into alignment before the fullness of what God wants to happen can be fulfilled. The three things are: God's Will, God's Way and God's When. You must know what God wants you to do. You must know how He intends for it to come to pass. You must be in sync with His calendar and timetable.

Here are some points to consider re timing:

(a) Is it for right now? Does God have or do you know you have to do some preliminary things before it is time for you to move forward? For example, do you need to improve your education or re-arrange your finances or other resources? You might need to get out of debt by downsizing your house.

(b) Ask the Lord for and wait until you get the confirmations you need for major decisions.

When my wife Lynne and I were considering moving interstate, we had every kind of confirmation, including Scriptures, inner witness, prophetic words and the alignment of circumstances. More recently, when I handed over my church to my associate pastor in order to focus on writing and inter-church and international ministry, I had the consensus of our local and denominational overseers, the inner witness and still, small voice of the Lord and some amazing prophetic confirmations. A visiting Indian prophet named the year of service I was in (my thirty-second. He literally saw the number 32) and the names of my two daughters. That was a miraculous confirmation of the timing of the Lord for our transition.

(c) Don't be rushed into making a decision you are not sure about.

(xi)   Ask yourself: Have I got the right partners, or the wrong ones?

Am I unequally yoked to unbelievers? (2 Corinthians 6:14). Do my partners have resources and skills that I need? Have I known my potential partners long enough to have built up trust based on their proven integrity and performance?

(xii)   Can you see the Hand of God leading you in a certain direction? Are doors open or closed, opening or closing?

Use discernment to understand if God is with you or trying to stop you (as He did Balaam in Numbers 22:21-34); or, if the evil one is hindering you (as he did Paul in 1 Thessalonians 2:18); or, if people are pressuring you to do their will, not God's; or, if you are simply being selfish.

Get Godly wisdom and make good decisions

You must resist the devil and press on, knowing the Lord is with you to help you overcome every obstacle and succeed in the mission He has appointed you to fulfil. Don't expect the enemy to flee from you in the first round of every battle. (James 4:7).

Sometimes we try to convince ourselves that a decision is the Lord's Will, just because we want to do it. That is how many Christians take the Lord's Name in vain. They say the Lord told me to do this or that, when He didn't.

Overcoming: Faith Food Snack Pack

What is one thing you have learned from this teaching?

What is one thing you can do to implement this teaching?

Faith Declaration:

Lord I thank You for Your Word and Your Holy Spirit living in me and the wisdom of God You make available and known to me. I put myself, my mind, my relationships and partnerships and my decisions fully into Your Hands. I ask You to guide me into Your perfect will in every area of my life. I declare the riches of Your grace are coming to me as I make Spirit-led decisions that attract Your favour and Divine Partnership. I confess success and prosperity and all the benefits of operating with the wisdom of God are mine, in Jesus Name. Amen.

8
3 Kinds of Forgiveness

Be kind and compassionate to one another, forgiving each other, just as in Christ God forgave you.
Ephesians 4:32

Throughout history there have been amazing examples of forgiveness.

- God forgave Paul, who called himself "the worst of sinners" in 1 Timothy 1:15-16. The Bible says that without Christ, we were not only sinners, but God's enemies. (Romans 5:8-10).

- On Tuesday 27 January 2015, the online *Daily Mail* Australia ran an article headed: "Could you forgive your rapist, your father for murdering your mother or a drunk driver for killing your husband? These brave women did..." It went on to share the stories of the four women, including Joanne Nodding and Natalia Aggiano, who were involved in those terrible real-life incidents.

- Uchendi Nwani was the stepson of a prominent Baptist pastor in Nashville. He lived a double life as a serious drug dealer while still at school. After he was arrested and served time in jail, Uchendi came out of prison carrying his Bible, with the goal of making his parents proud. He is now a multi-millionaire barber-school owner, who has helped many at-risk youth and supported church prison programmes.

These examples illustrate the three kinds of forgiveness we all need to implement in our lives.

(i) Receiving forgiveness from God for our sins.

It is important to understand that we never forgive God for anything, because He is perfect and never does any wrong. No matter what we think God should have done or not done or stopped from happening, He is infinitely good, wise and holy. He never makes mistakes. He always has our best interests at heart, because He is motivated by the highest form of love that is possible to experience and express, the (Greek) "agape" love of God.

The Rock! His work is perfect, for all His ways are just; a God of faithfulness and without injustice, righteous and upright is He.

Deuteronomy 32:4 NAS

The second important matter to understand is that we do not just confess our sins once when we get saved and never again. I am shocked by people who teach an error concerning the fact that the sacrifice and triumph of Jesus was for all sin, for all people, for all time.

Their error is that they say all our sins past, present and future were washed away by the Blood of Jesus on the cross. Therefore, we do not need to confess our sins other than when we first get saved, because they are all forgiven.

Let me illustrate what I believe: Imagine you won a year's supply of groceries. You go to the store to collect your prize. You take everything you want. The next day you realise that in your excitement, as you selected so many treats you normally would have not taken, you forgot a couple of essential things. Will the items somehow self-deliver themselves to your door? No, they won't. Do you have to go back to the store to get what you didn't take the first trip? Yes, you will have to go back to the store and explain to the people that you didn't take all to which you were entitled.

Similarly, when we get saved, we ask the Lord to forgive all the sins we have committed up to that point in our lives. How can we ask Him to forgive sins we haven't committed, sins we don't even know that we will commit? The fact is that we do need to confess our future sins, but only at the time we commit them, or after, definitely not before.

Even though the Lord does know in advance that we will commit our future sins and He has provided for our forgiveness, we cannot ask for forgiveness of something that hasn't happened.

We can only confess and be forgiven of sins we have already committed. Therefore after we are saved, we must continue to repent of and ask forgiveness for sins we commit in the course of our life.

In John 13:1-17, Jesus taught the apostles to let Him wash their feet.

> *Jesus replied, "A person who has bathed all over does not need to wash, except for the feet, to be entirely clean.*
>
> *John 13:10*

3 Kinds of forgiveness

The spiritual meaning of this verse is that after you are saved (bathed), you need only to deal with the daily impact of the dirt of this world on your life. So, let's take the advice of the apostle John who was there that night with Jesus.

> *If we claim to be without sin, we deceive ourselves and the truth is not in us. ⁹ If we confess our sins, He is faithful and just and will forgive us our sins and purify us from all unrighteousness.*
>
> *1 John 1:8-9*

(ii) The second kind of forgiveness is us forgiving others who have hurt or offended us.

It is impossible to go through life without experiencing hurts, wounds and disappointments. Some people's responses to these lead to depression, unforgiveness, breakdown of relationships, resentment and bitterness.

Jesus challenges and empowers us to love our critics, wrong-doers and even our enemies. (Luke 6:27-36).

Forgiving those who offend us is never easy, but it is a choice we can, should and indeed we must make. The New Testament makes it clear that, if we do not forgive others, then God will not forgive us. (Matthew 6:14-15).

The Lord always gives us the ability, by His Holy Spirit, to live according to His Word and example.

Without forgiving others, you will not be healed of the soul damage and the inner negatives of hurt, anger, resentment, bitterness or prejudice that offences inflict upon us.

Without forgiving others, you will not be healed of the soul damage and the inner negatives of hurt, anger, resentment, bitterness or prejudice that offences inflict upon us.

With forgiveness, there must also be the refusal to remember (or discuss) the offence any more. Keeping it alive in your memory, or in your mouth, keeps the pain alive in your soul.

The source of this quote is unknown, but I agree with its principles. "The first to apologise is the bravest. The first to forgive is the strongest. And the first to forget is the happiest."

(iii)   The third area of forgiveness is that of forgiving ourselves.

3 Kinds of forgiveness

There is therefore now no condemnation for those who are in Christ Jesus.

Romans 8:1

We can learn from our mistakes. We can do better next time. We need to give ourselves time to heal. There is a time gap between when you forgive yourself (and others) by faith and when your emotions catch up with your faith.

We have to do the same as the Lord does with our sins. We have to choose to not remember them anymore.

Possibly the greatest examples of this are the apostles Peter and Paul, Mary Magdalene and the woman of Samaria. They all had much about which to forgive themselves.

Every time Peter heard a rooster crow after Jesus' death must have reminded him of his sin of denying his Lord and friend. Yet Peter was able to move forward with his life and ministry without carrying the baggage of lingering guilt or shame or regret.

Paul was also able to leave his negative past behind, even though he described himself as the worst of sinners. (1 Timothy 1:15; Philippians 3:12-14).

Mary Magdalene had seven demons. What sinful, even Satanic, things had she experienced that had brought her into such captivity of the devil? Yet she was so close to the Lord, because she lived in the freedom of His forgiveness and healing.

The woman of Samaria had five husbands and a defacto. What a walking relationship disaster she was. I believe she was sexually abused as a child. Thereafter, she allowed men to use and mistreat her.

She was so ashamed of her past and present and so conscious of the judgement of her fellow villagers that she went to the well in the heat of the day to avoid the rejection and scorn of her peers. She refused to go at the same time as they went to the well. It's possible that she could have been shunned not only because of the unacceptability of her defacto relationship in the culture of that day, but also because other women did not trust her to get to know their husbands.

After Jesus came into her life, she turned into an instant evangelist, shouting His praises to all of her neighbours. She was able to forgive the men, her critics and herself and move into a ministry of influence. Hallelujah. What a mighty Saviour and Lord we have.

Don't keep focussing on your past mistakes, even if the latest one was only yesterday or an hour ago.

Put it under the Blood. Fix it in whatever way you can.

Receive your forgiveness and healing. Move on. Don't keep beating yourself up because, when you do, you are doing the devil's job for him. When he comes to accuse you send him packing in Jesus' Name.

Don't do the devil's work by condemning yourself. When he accuses you, send him packing in Jesus' Name.

---

^{10} Then I heard a loud voice in heaven say: "Now have come the salvation and the power and the kingdom of our God, and the authority of his Messiah. For the accuser of our brothers and sisters, who accuses them before our God day and night, has been hurled down. ^{11} They triumphed over him by the blood of the Lamb and by the word of their testimony; they did not love their lives so much as to shrink from death.

Revelation 12:11

To overcome the devil's accusations you must first accept that your sins are indeed washed away by the Blood of the Lamb. Just as the Lord does not remember our sins any more (Isaiah 43:25), we have to choose to accept our forgiveness and do the same as Him. This does not require us to get a case of amnesia, because God surely doesn't have amnesia. He simply chooses to put the sins He has forgiven out of His mind. That's what you need to do. Every time the memory of the sin comes into your mind, replace it with thoughts of something else. Rebuke it as coming from the devil, the accuser. Don't think of the accusation as coming from yourself and certainly not from God, because He has put it out of His Mind.

Secondly, speak out loud the word of your testimony that you are a saint, not a sinner; that you have been saved by grace; that your sins are under the Blood; that you are forgiven; that you are the righteousness of God in Christ. Amen.

> *Submit yourselves, then, to God. Resist the devil, and he will flee from you.*
> *James 4:7*

In order to overcome the accusations of the devil, you have to do two things. Firstly, submit to what God in His Word says about you. Remember this: You cannot resist both God and the devil at the same time. If you try to do that, you will be in a situation as if the walls are closing in on you from both sides. When you submit to God, you and He are now on the same side, pushing in the same direction against the devil and against sin, shame, guilt, sickness, depression and every evil thing. Secondly, resist the devil with the Word of God and in every spiritual way until he flees from you. Be aware that he is not likely to run away after only one skirmish.

Thirdly, understand what "loving not" your life is all about and do that. It does not mean (a) not living your full life span; or (b) not enjoying your life. It is about losing your life in the service of your Saviour and King, Jesus. That is ultimate satisfaction. You overcome condemnation by faith in what the Word of God says about you and by active faith in the form of doing the good works He prepared in advance for you to do. (Ephesians 2:10).

What is one thing you have learned from this teaching?

What is one thing you can do to implement this teaching?

Faith Declaration

I thank You Lord because You, Who are so perfectly holy, have forgiven me and clothed me with the righteousness of God in Christ. I am grateful that You have forgiven me all my sins, big and small, no matter how many of them there were. I praise You for the fact that Jesus has taken my punishment for my sins and enables me, by Your Word and Spirit, to break the power of sin in my life. I thank You for helping me forgive others and be healed of the hurts I felt and the bad attitudes I developed because of what happened. I declare in Jesus' Name that I am forgiven, healed and set free from my own feelings of guilt, shame, anger and depression. I praise You because You have enabled me to overcome the accusations and condemnation of the devil and criticisms of people. I rejoice in You, because You enable me to walk forward in my life with You, cleansed from and free of all my previous sins, in Jesus' Name. Amen. Hallelujah.

Overcoming: Faith Food Snack Pack

Faith

9

What is Faith? It is the confident assurance that something we want is going to happen. It is the certainty that what we hope for is waiting for us even though we cannot see it up ahead.

Hebrews 11:1 Living Bible

Now faith is the assurance (the confirmation, the title deed) of the things [we] hope for, being the proof of things [we] do not see and the conviction of their reality [faith perceiving as real fact what is not revealed to the senses].

Hebrews 11:1 AMP

Only Faith can guarantee the blessings we hope for or prove the existence of realities that at present remain unseen.

Hebrews 11:1 Jerusalem Bible

Saint Augustine said: "Faith is to believe what we do not see; and the reward of this faith is to see what we believe." He must have read Mark 11:22-24.

During a time of severe drought, a church called an emergency prayer meeting to pray for rain. The ones who had real faith brought an umbrella with them.

What is Faith?

- Faith is a confident expectation of God's promises coming to pass.
- Faith is being assured that the things we expect, due to what the Lord has said, will indeed happen.
- Faith is being convinced about things that have not happened yet, and therefore remain unseen.

(i) F-aith is:

Founded on God, meaning, on His nature and abilities.

When a person truly believes that God is the all-powerful, always-good and grace-giving Lord Who willingly and abundantly provides for our every need and righteous desire, then all things become possible.

A man walked too near the edge of a cliff. As he fell, he grabbed hold of a branch and held on for dear life. Every time he heard any kind of sound, he would call out: "Help, is there anybody up there?"

Faith

For a long while no-one replied, because the sounds he heard were just the wind blowing the branches, small stones and other loose things on the cliff top. Finally, the man heard a Voice call back: "It's going to be OK. I am God. Trust Me and let go of the branch and I will save you." After a time of thinking about what the Voice said, the man cried out: "Is there anybody else up there?"

That man did not trust the Nature or Voice or Ability of God.

(ii)   f-A-ith is:

Active confidence in God and His Word.

Christian Faith is not just accepting that the Bible is true. It is acting in accordance with what the Bible says. Some time ago, Holy Spirit said to me: When you do what the Bible says, God will do what the Bible says.

When you do what the Bible says, God will do what the Bible says

Faith is Active:

The just shall live by faith
Romans 1.17

Christians live according to Biblical principles every day of their lives. They trust in and rely on God in every area of life.

Faith without works is dead
James 2:17

Faith is knowing the will of God and doing it.

Faith is hearing the voice of God and obeying it.

True Christians are fully obedient to God, His Word and His Spirit. They do this willingly and cheerfully, because they love the Lord, not because of a sense of legalistic or religious duty.

Faith is Active Confidence:

Our faith makes possible all that is possible with God. (Mark 9.23; Matthew 19.26).

Believers expect God to answer prayer and fulfil the promises of His Word.

Evangelist, author and speaker Kevin Dedmon preached in our church. He expressed his faith, expectancy and confidence in God during one of his messages by saying: "When I pray, God comes and does good things."

Faith

I have a plaque on my desk that says: "Faith is not believing God can – it is knowing that He will."

Believers expect God to be willing to do good and great things.

The incident of Jesus telling the leper He was willing to heal him and then doing the miracle the man requested, was inserted into the Bible by Holy Spirit in order to teach us how willing God is!

(iii)   fa-I-th is:

being In love with and In touch with the Lord.

We learn to put our faith in God by building an intimate, personal, daily relationship with Him.

We are King's kids, the adopted sons and daughters of God. Our sonship is the source of our blessing, inheritance and authority in Christ.

Think about this: If the father said yes to his rebellious, self-centred prodigal son, how much more will God our Heavenly Father say yes to you who want to please Him? Matthew and Luke both tell us that our Heavenly Father wants to bless His children "much more" than good, earthly fathers do. (Matthew 7.11; Luke 11.13).

> *... people who know their God will be strong and take action.*
>
> *Daniel 11:32b ISV*

The Hebrew word for "know" in this verse indicates intimate knowledge. When a Christian knows the Lord intimately, he becomes strong in the Lord and in the power of His might. His faith grows strong and he takes faith actions that lead to great exploits happening that bring glory to God and victory and blessing to His people.

(iv)   fai-T-h is:

Total trust, as a little child in her perfect heavenly Father.

If you've ever seen a puppy roll over on her back for a tummy rub, then you have seen a picture of total trust and complete, willing, loving vulnerability.

We are to trust God even when our mind just does not and even cannot understand what is going on or why certain things are not happening.

> *Trust in the Lord with all your heart and lean not on your own understanding.*
>
> *Proverbs 3:5*

There are times when we must simply be still and know that He is God (Ps. 46:10a), because there's nothing else we can do.

Faith

These are times when we truly must walk by faith and not by sight. (2 Corinthians 5:7).

The key to total trust in God is to know beyond any shadow of a doubt that God is good and great all the time; that He is always with you and for you, not against you; and that the Lord will never hurt you, leave you, fail you, nor forget you.

(v)   Fait-H is:

Holding on to God and His Word, no matter what, nor how long it takes for your miracle to become a reality in our material world. Remember, if you have claimed your miracle, your blessing, your inheritance by faith, based on the promises of God's Word, then, it already is a reality in the spiritual world of the Kingdom of God.

The Lord told Joshua He had already given the Promised Land to the new leader of Israel. But Joshua and the Jews still had to possess the land in order to make real on earth what God said was already real in His spiritual kingdom.

Hebrews 6:12b tells us that faith and patience, which are known in a more active form of expression as "persistence", are often both required in order to inherit the promises of God.

> *You need to persevere so that when you have done the will of God, you will receive what He has promised.*
>
> *Hebrews 10:36*

Years ago, Holy Spirit taught me that persistence overcomes enemy resistance. So keep on believing. Keep on doing what God wants you to do and the devil will not be able to rob you of your due season harvest or your appointed time miracle.

Be steadfast in prayer, understanding that faith is Forwarding All Items To Heaven. Jesus Himself said: Everyone who asks, receives. (Matthew 7:8a). Don't just pray in a religious, casual, half-hearted way. The words "ask" and "receive" in Greek are strong, not weak, words.

Prayer is asking with conviction, based on the knowledge that the covenant has been fully paid for by Jesus. Therefore, the benefits of the covenant are a done deal.

The word Jesus used for "receive" is a military word that means "seize" the answer. We don't pray and passively wait for the answer for years. We sow into the answer, the harvest, by practical active faith. We take the opportunities that come our way and we create our own. We position ourselves to receive a miracle and to be a miracle

Faith

What is one thing you have learned from this teaching?

_____

What is one thing you can do to implement this teaching

_____

Faith Declaration

Lord I praise You because You are good and great. I thank You for rewarding my active faith. I declare that by Your grace my miracle will soon be manifest. I receive it by faith and speak it into being in Jesus' mighty Name. Amen. I thank You Lord for Your love for me. I know You always want what is best for me. I bring every thought of mine captive to the obedience of Christ and of Your Word. I declare my complete trust in You for my every need, godly desire and faith goal. I believe every resource, blessing and miracle will be manifest in my life soon, because Jesus has said "Yes" to every Bible promise. I now say the "Amen" in His Name. I declare that my faith, patience and persistence will be richly rewarded, because God's Word is true and Jesus is Lord. Amen.

ABOUT THE AUTHOR

 Nick Watson has been happily married to Lynne since 1970. They have 3 children, Kylie, Simon and Rebekah; 4 (so far) grandchildren Katie, Rennick, Craig and Aiden; and 1 great-granddaughter, Riley.

Nick is the Founder, Principal Prophet, Author and Teacher, and People Builder of Prophetic Power Ministries.

He was for years the Senior Pastor of Bayside Christian Family (Apostolic) Church, a thriving Spirit-filled church in Brisbane, Queensland. Australia.

Nick has been a recognised prophet in the Apostolic Church Australia for more than 25 years. He has served in various denominational leadership roles.

Nick has preached and prophesied throughout Australia and overseas, with a signs-following ministry.

YOUR FEEDBACK

If this book "Overcoming: Faith Food Snack Pack" has encouraged your faith, please share your testimony with us at the email address below.

CONTACT Nick Watson

If you desire to contact Nick concerning a ministry engagement at your church, group, camp or leaders event please visit our website:

www.youcanprophesy.com

 www.facebook.com/nickjwatson.ycp

email: youcanprophesy@gmail.com

OTHER BOOKS by Nick Watson

Faith Food Snack Pack – Healthy Soul

Faith Food Snack Pack – Good News

Faith Food Snack Pack – Holy Spirit

Lessons From My Dog – 33 Faith Lifters

You Can Prophesy – Supernatural. Simple. Safe.

www.ingramcontent.com/pod-product-compliance
Lightning Source LLC
Chambersburg PA
CBHW072054290426
44110CB00014B/1682